T0058173

THE POCKET GUIDE TO

Bad Boyfriends

THE POCKET GUIDE TO

Bad Boyfriends

How to identify 40 types of boys gone wrong

Ruby Turner
Illustrated by Simon Coleman

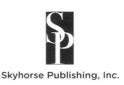

Skyhorse Publishing, Inc.

Skyhorse Publishing books may be purchased in bulk at special discounts
for sales promotion, corporate gifts, fund-raising, or educational purposes.
Special editions can also be created to specifications. For details, contact
the Special Sales Department, Skyhorse Publishing, 307 West 36th Street,
11th Floor, New York, NY 10018 or info@skyhorsepublishing.com.

Skyhorse® and Skyhorse Publishing® are registered trademarks
of Skyhorse Publishing, Inc.®, a Delaware corporation.

Visit our website at www.skyhorsepublishing.com.

10 9 8 7 6 5 4 3 2 1

Library of Congress Cataloging-in-Publication Data is available on file.

Special thanks to my amazing editor Mariela Quintana
Cover design by Simon Coleman

Print ISBN: 978-1-5107-5636-6
Ebook ISBN: 978-1-5107-5637-3

Printed in China

Contents

"I'm no cupid, stupid!"

Introduction

Why is it so hard to meet the right guy? You've got all the apps, but despite all the swiping (and all the dating!), none of the guys you meet really clicks. Maybe it's not working because DJ Devil is in the booth, spinning the tracks that keep us all dating a long list of Mr. Wrongs in the search for Mr. Right.

You might even date DJ Devil. You'll know it the moment you meet a guy you can't get enough of. He's the itch you can't scratch; the one who takes you to places you didn't know existed; the one you can't hold on to but can never forget. Just remember, he's not a keeper.

But sometimes even the Devil takes a night off, allowing you to let the right one in. Enter The Keeper, your one true love. He's out there somewhere, but finding him takes time and a lot of hands on research (fun), broken hearts (no fun), and sleepless nights (some of those were really fun!).

The Starter Set

These are your first loves in all their horny, hormone-addled, pimple-riddled glory. Remember The Parents' Favorite (your parents turned out to be more into him than you were), The Party Animal (into keg parties, crowds, and fun), and The Lead Guitarist (into himself)? First love! Always short, often sweet, and sometimes crazy.

The Parents' Favorite
The Starter Set

WHY YOU FELL FOR HIM

He was so responsible and well-adjusted! He had a 401(k), went to the dentist twice a year, and ate three balanced meals a day. He totally had his act together—submitting his tax return in January and offering to do yours for you.

WHY YOU SPLIT UP

Someone sensible and practical was your parents' dream, not yours. They loved him more than you ever did.

DESCRIPTION

From the side part to the sensible shoes, he is decked out in J.Crew—except in winter when he shows off his large collection of scratchy, hand-knitted sweaters.

NOT TO BE CONFUSED WITH

Too Into Your Mom, The Young Fogey, The Nerd.

CHECKLIST

Briefcase welded to right hand; owns a pants press ✓

International standard bridge player, Eagle Scout ✓

Agrees with your father on everything; compliments your mother ✓

Your parents measure every future boyfriend against him ✓

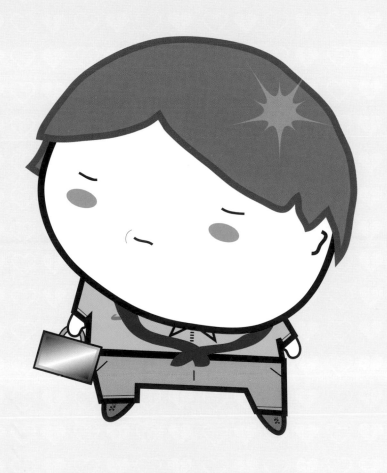

"Dinner was just delicious, Mrs. Jones."

The Party Animal

The Starter Set

WHY YOU FELL FOR HIM

At last, someone who let you be your wild and crazy self! You could dance like no one was watching, drink shots all night, sleep all day, then wake up and do it again.

WHY YOU SPLIT UP

Your company alone wasn't enough. He always had to be at a party. Did alone time with The Party Animal bore you, or did you (and your liver) just get sick of having fun all the time? Whatever…

DESCRIPTION

Baseball cap, board shorts, and Dunks. Looks like he's slept in his clothes. Because he has. All that beer is starting to show on his waistline.

NOT TO BE CONFUSED WITH

The Jock, The Alcoholic.

CHECKLIST

Knows about every house party in the tristate area ✓

Thinks that burgers, fries, and nachos are the three main food groups ✓

Has a sixth sense for when to show up (and leave) a party ✓

Up for bottomless brunches, cocktails, keg parties, all-night raves, etc. ✓

"Party on, dude!"

The Jock

The Starter Set

WHY YOU FELL FOR HIM

The most popular guy in school. The smell of Axe. That six-pack! That tight ass! The way he made you feel light as a feather—finally shower sex was as much fun as it looked in the movies.

WHY YOU SPLIT UP

Festering bags of sweaty exercise clothes, endless special diets, always hanging out with the team, and watching ESPN nonstop were bad enough but the "no sex before the big game" rule was the deal breaker.

DESCRIPTION

Letter jacket, class ring, team mascot tattoo. Could be Superman's body double.

NOT TO BE CONFUSED WITH

The Party Animal, The Prom King.

CHECKLIST

Protein shakes for breakfast, lunch, and dinner ✓

Able to watch three or four sporting events at once ✓

American Pie could be a biopic about him ✓

Always has time for the team–you, not so much ✓

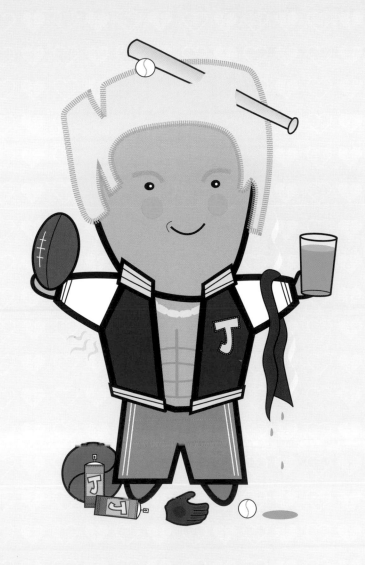

"You know I want to, but Coach says we can't."

The Lead Guitarist

The Starter Set

WHY YOU FELL FOR HIM

From the moment you saw him, you were instantly smitten—that messy hair, those low-slung jeans, the big dilated pupils! He made you feel like you were sixteen.

WHY YOU SPLIT UP

You got tired of having to pay for everything and going to bars where everyone else really was sixteen. And you couldn't stand having a boyfriend whose waist was smaller than yours.

DESCRIPTION

Tousled, just-got-out-of-bed look. You can see his undies above the tight jeans. Band T-shirts, vintage leather jacket, and beat-up Converse All Stars form his capsule wardrobe.

NOT TO BE CONFUSED WITH

The Party Animal, The Perennial Teenager.

CHECKLIST

Extensive record collection and guitar but only knows three chords

Cigarette tucked behind one ear; drinks Jack and Coke

So self-absorbed he forgets your number, your email, and your name

Never has cash; always has his weed pen and backstage passes

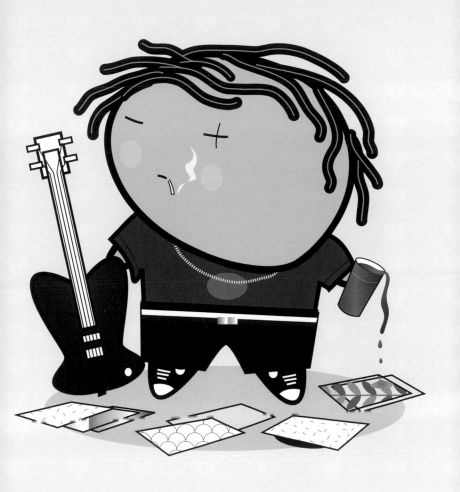

"You've never heard of the Cardiacs?!"

Too Into Your Mom

The Starter Set

WHY YOU FELL FOR HIM

When you brought him home, he fit right in. And your mom really liked him, which made for a nice change. He was so helpful, always offering to clear the table and do the dishes.

WHY YOU SPLIT UP

He said your mom was smart and fun (true), then that she was cute, and had a great figure—whoa! He had to go! You knew you had made the right decision when he kept "bumping into" your mom at Starbucks for months afterward.

DESCRIPTION

Follows your mom around like a puppy. Laughs like a hyena at your mom's bad jokes. Shaves off his beard and cuts his hair when your mom mentions she doesn't like the shaggy look.

NOT TO BE CONFUSED WITH

The Parents' Favorite, The Needy Guy.

CHECKLIST

Late night heart-to-hearts with your mom in the kitchen ✓

His favorite movie: *The Graduate* ✓

Hints your Dad isn't good enough and your parents should split up ✓

Surprises your mom with little gifts, flowers, and candy ✓

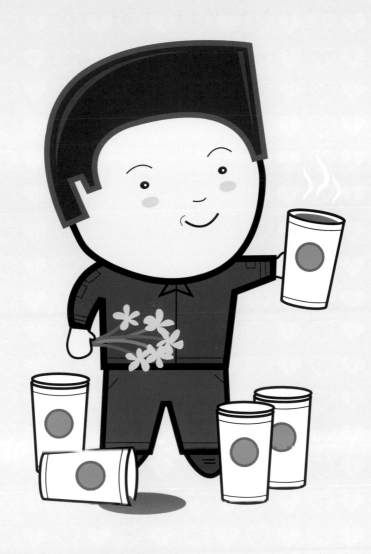

"Can I help in the kitchen?"

Weirdos and Losers

Some of these guys turned out to be too kooky to care about (The Collector), while others should have come with a government health warning (The Stalker). You had fun playing doctors and nurses with The Hypochondriac, but The Jealous Guy was just too weird with his controlling ways. In the end, none of them hit the spot—especially Mr. Sad in the Sack, who failed to even find it in the first place.

The Fixer Upper

Weirdos and Losers

WHY YOU FELL FOR HIM

Not the most dynamic guy, but with a little help from you, he could be perfect. There were just a few things that needed to change, like his hair, his clothes, his job, his home, his laugh…

WHY YOU SPLIT UP

You casually made a Pinterest page of menswear to inspire him. And then signed him up to get push notifications every time you added to it. You downloaded the Indeed app, but he never bothered to even apply for the job. Then he changed his phone's password. After that, you deleted him from everything. The end.

DESCRIPTION

He's your basic bro. The one in plaid with brown hair at the bar. No, not that one. The guy next to that one. Oy. He needs something to set him apart!

NOT TO BE CONFUSED WITH

The Momma's Boy, The Couch Potato.

CHECKLIST

Apartment furnished by one-stop-shopping at Ikea

Actually prefers the house wine

Eats the same three dinners on rotation. All of them feature hamburger

Drives his grandma's old Honda Civic

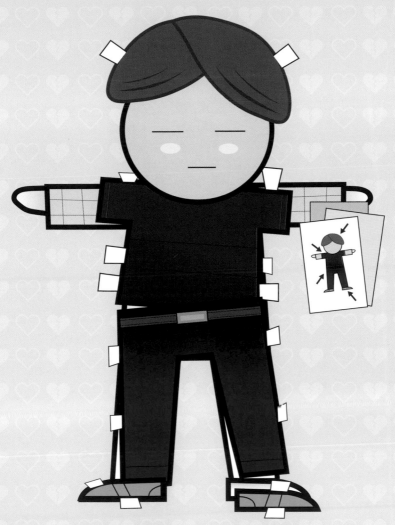

"But I like it the way it is."

The Couch Potato

Weirdos and Losers

WHY YOU FELL FOR HIM

He was super cuddly and really chill. Like a big teddy bear. You loved spending time with him curled up on the couch watching Netflix.

WHY YOU SPLIT UP

After a couple of months, you'd finished *GOT* and *Stranger Things* and every season of *Bob's Burgers*. You were both stuck in a rut but you were the only one who got off the couch. Your Couch Potato wouldn't budge.

DESCRIPTION

His spirit animal is the sloth. He actually wears the Snuggie his mom gave him for his birthday. Every day.

NOT TO BE CONFUSED WITH

The Big Lebowski, The Gamer.

CHECKLIST

Huge, super comfy leather couch ✔

Giant TV. Subscribes to the full package and every streaming service going ✔

Takeout for breakfast, lunch, and dinner are his idea of heaven ✔

Gets his clothes from Amazon Prime ✔

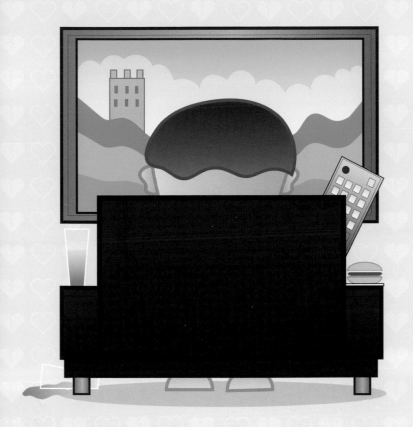

"Let's stay in and watch this box set."

Mr. Sad in the Sack

Weirdos and Losers

WHY YOU FELL FOR HIM

Whatever you liked about him was overshadowed by what happened when you took him home. Nothing worth talking about. And yet, you couldn't stop talking to your girlfriends about it! You all agreed he could learn and that you were the one to teach him.

WHY YOU SPLIT UP

When you suggested slowing things down and enjoying the moment, he told you that foreplay was for girls (he got that right!). He thought going down was a one-way street and sex was missionary all the way unless you were interested in anal. You weren't. He said you were no fun.

DESCRIPTION

His noisy huffing and puffing in bed doesn't set you on fire but it is over so quickly you're not sure anything happened at all.

NOT TO BE CONFUSED WITH

The Fixer Upper, An Eggplant Emoji (Not).

CHECKLIST

Insists on scented condoms ✓

Has a nickname for his penis ✓

Falls asleep on top of you afterward ✓

Washes his sheets semi-annually ✓

"That was awesome!"

The Mansplainer

Weirdos and Losers

WHY YOU FELL FOR HIM

At first, you thought it was confidence. He seemed to know so much! He even told you how YOU felt about everything from your favorite wine to your period pains. Cool. Thanks, dude.

WHY YOU SPLIT UP

He insisted on explaining everything to you including how the stock market works, gravity, and what Gloria Steinem really meant. Going out to the movies was a nightmare—he'd go over the plot until 2:00 a.m. And that was for rom-coms. When he explained childbirth to your best friend who'd just had twins, that was the last straw.

DESCRIPTION

Bow tie and horn-rimmed glasses, carefully curated moustache, constantly chirping Apple Watch. Pompous expression.

NOT TO BE CONFUSED WITH

The Sexist, The Connoisseur.

CHECKLIST

Owns a flip chart and a set of Sharpies, and he's not afraid to use them ✔

Walks around with a Bluetooth headset to call his mom in case no one else will listen ✔

Thinks he knows more about your body than your gynecologist ✔

Never stops talking, just in case someone else gets a word in ✔

"Oh, I can explain…"

The Gamer

Weirdos and Losers

WHY YOU FELL FOR HIM

He was super competitive, and so were you. You liked playing games, and so did he. You met at Comic Con and thought between the furry cosplay costume, his obsession with multiplayer video games, and his addiction to live streaming on Twitch, there was potential for some serious kink.

WHY YOU SPLIT UP

You thought your Lara Croft getup would really turn him on. Turned out he preferred the minions in *Minecraft*. Eventually you gave up on waiting for him to beat the next level and left him in search of real world stuff like food, sleep, and yes, sex.

DESCRIPTION

Dark circles under his eyes, pasty skin, blue hair, braided beard, large collection of game-themed T-shirts.

NOT TO BE CONFUSED WITH

The Couch Potato, The IT Guy.

CHECKLIST

Minecraft tattoos on his forearms ✔

Spends hours watching Ninja play *Fortnite* on Twitch ✔

Once fired for falling asleep at work ✔

On first-name terms with the pizza delivery guy ✔

"I'm in the zone."

Midlife Crisis Man

Weirdos and Losers

WHY YOU FELL FOR HIM

This guy was no silver fox, but he did have a ton of cash and liked to spend it on two things: you and his new motorcycle. While the biker getup was contrived, at least the helmet hid his bald spot.

WHY YOU SPLIT UP

It was sort of funny when your friends called him Dad, but beyond weird when you did. And he wouldn't stop talking about his ex-wife, his messy divorce, and his 401(k).

DESCRIPTION

He's got all the biker gear, but on him it's all wrong. Maybe it's the little belly over the tight leathers, that gray hair in the goatee, or just the fact that it's all brand new?

NOT TO BE CONFUSED WITH

The Two-Timer, The Boss.

CHECKLIST

A Peloton bike he never uses ✓

A pack of cigarettes he only smokes with you ✓

Viagra, for real, not for recreation ✓

Black American Express Card; red motorcycle helmet ✓

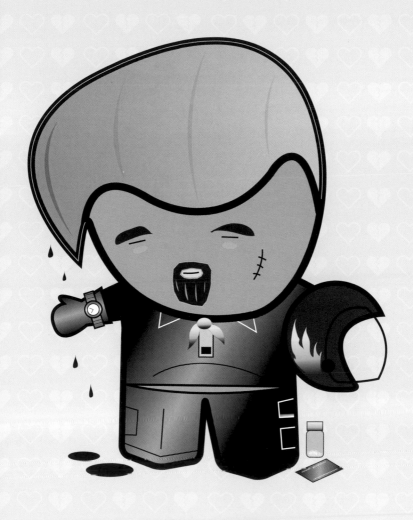

"The kids are with the ex tonight."

The Neat Freak

Weirdos and Losers

WHY YOU FELL FOR HIM

He had great taste and bags of style and he loved shopping. Not only did he look great all the time but his apartment was so perfect it was like staying in a hotel. Almost eerily sterile.

WHY YOU SPLIT UP

If you touched anything in his apartment, he moved it a millimeter to get it back into position. If you put a coffee cup into his dishwasher, he reloaded it so it was "right." He woke you up by vacuuming in the middle of the night. He showered after sex. And flossed. Which made you feel dirty, but not in a good way. When he told you your apartment wasn't clean enough, you told him where to go.

DESCRIPTION

Clean inside and out: has his teeth whitened, his eyebrows shaped, a full wax, and even colonic irrigation. Yuck.

NOT TO BE CONFUSED WITH

The Nerd, An Old Lady, Mr. Clean.

CHECKLIST

Finds ironing therapeutic ✔

Combs the fringes on his throw rugs so they are straight ✔

Organizes his books by color and size ✔

Insists he doesn't have OCD, then goes to wash his hands–again ✔

"Wait! Don't touch that!"

The Stalker

Weirdos and Losers

WHY YOU FELL FOR HIM

You can't remember because it got so weird, but the gifts should have been a sign. First, it was a teddy bear (cute), a clock (hmm), a smoke detector (over-cautious). Then you got it: they were spy cams.

WHY YOU SPLIT UP

That doesn't matter anymore. It's what happened next. Did I mention the surveillance? The texts, calls, messages, and emails? Showing up at your work. At your mom's. At your grandma's. Is nothing sacred?

DESCRIPTION

Hat to hide face (who does he think he's fooling?). Lockpicks. Binoculars. Hidden camera. Voice recorder pen. All nicely accessorized with the brand new restraining order you got him.

NOT TO BE CONFUSED WITH

The Jealous Guy, The Needy Guy.

CHECKLIST

Shops at The Spy Store; thinks he's James Bond ✓

Loves camo gear, steaming open mail, GPS trackers ✓

Hates new boyfriends, any evidence you have a life ✓

Models himself on Dirty John ✓

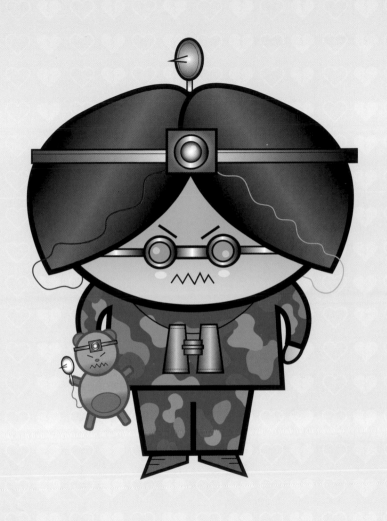

"I just want to be with you..."

The Jealous Guy

Weirdos and Losers

WHY YOU FELL FOR HIM

He took such good care of you! Maybe he even rescued you from something. When you felt vulnerable, he vowed to protect you forever (and ever and ever). The big weirdo.

WHY YOU SPLIT UP

When he didn't want your hairdresser "playing that way with your hair," you realized he'd crossed the line between "loving and protective" and "obsessive and freaky."

DESCRIPTION

Worried frown, eyes darting from side to side checking out the possible competition. He's been known to carry a small telescope and a bugging device. You have been warned!

NOT TO BE CONFUSED WITH

The Stalker, Anger Management Class Boyfriend.

CHECKLIST

Needs to know where you are at all times–no matter what

Furtively reads your diary, bills, emails, text messages

Very, very insecure

Believes you can't do anything by yourself. Ever.

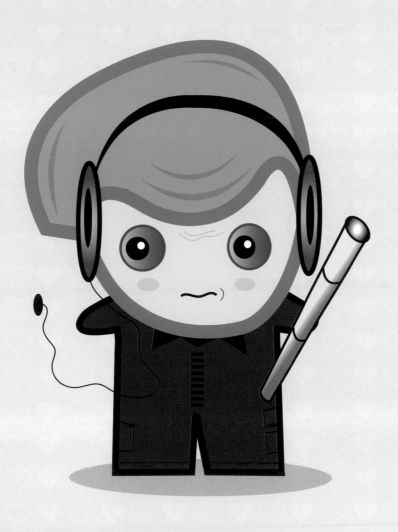

"I just happened to see this text..."

The Collector

Weirdos and Losers

WHY YOU FELL FOR HIM

You loved his enthusiasm. So much passion—if only it were directed at a person (you) rather than his obsession.

WHY YOU SPLIT UP

His collections + his weird hobbies = Hell, no! He thought soap carving/dumpster diving/antiquing were great date activities. You did not. He understood when you told him you couldn't see him anymore because your new hobby was faking your own death.

DESCRIPTION

Those aren't dust bunnies under his bed—that's his collection of Japanese polished dirt balls (hikaru dorodango). Don't open the closet, his collection of airline sickness bags will fall out. At least he doesn't collect "Love Dolls." Or is that why the garage is off limits?

NOT TO BE CONFUSED WITH

The Nerd, The Trekkie.

CHECKLIST

Collected stamps and coins then moved on to *Star Wars* figurines ✓

Hoards weird shit like Samurai swords, navel fluff, or snakeskins ✓

Owns every *Guinness World Records* book since 1985 ✓

If you ever want to sleep again, don't watch this old movie: *The Collector* ✓

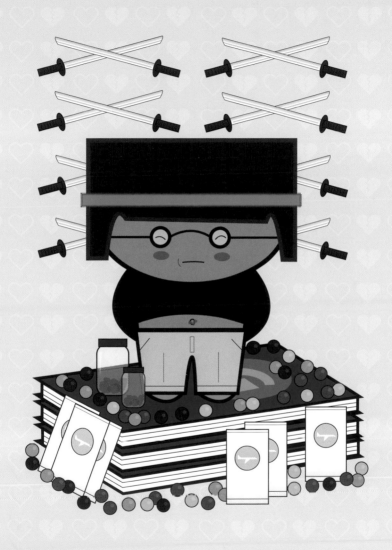

"My collection is nearly complete."

The Feeder

Weirdos and Losers

WHY YOU FELL FOR HIM

He spoiled you with boxes of macarons; baked mini cheesecakes with your name on them; had donuts sent to your doorstep, fed them to you in bed, then took you out for dinner. Life was sweet. Too sweet.

WHY YOU SPLIT UP

Big breakfasts, three-course lunches, tasty snacks, yummy suppers, midnight feasts—eating was a full-time job. After a while you realized that you were eating for the two of you. You fell out of love with him when your jeans no longer fit.

DESCRIPTION

Often seen at the stove wearing an apron; always wears a satisfied little smile as he watches you eat.

NOT TO BE CONFUSED WITH

The Chef, The Foodie.

CHECKLIST

Keeps a fully stocked picnic basket in his car

Has never seen a cake, pie, or cookie he didn't want you to try

Knows the location of all the best food trucks

Picks at his own dinner; insists you clean your plate

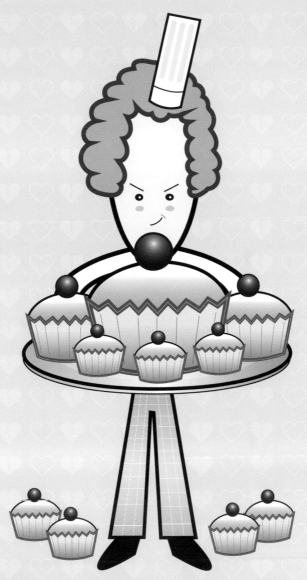

"Oh come on, just one more bite."

The Hypochondriac

Weirdos and Losers

WHY YOU FELL FOR HIM

He brought out the maternal instinct you didn't know you had with that sleepy, worried face. At first you thought all that time the two of you were spending in the bedroom was great, but then you realized it was all naps and back rubs (for him).

WHY YOU SPLIT UP

You caught him online in the middle of the night: Tinder? Porn? Nope, WebMD. You planned a romantic evening/weekend/vacation, but he canceled at the last minute: he didn't want to give you what he's got. Yuck! You didn't want it either. Or him.

DESCRIPTION

Furrowed brow. Often spotted clutching his latest source of pain, limping, or propped up in bed with a cool compress on his head.

NOT TO BE CONFUSED WITH

The Momma's Boy, The Needy Guy.

CHECKLIST

Fully stocked medicine cabinet

Kitchen stuffed with vitamins, supplements, superfoods, herbal teas

Hot water bottle, thermometer, large collection of ace bandages

Favorite TV shows: *House*, *ER*, *New Amsterdam*, *Grey's Anatomy*

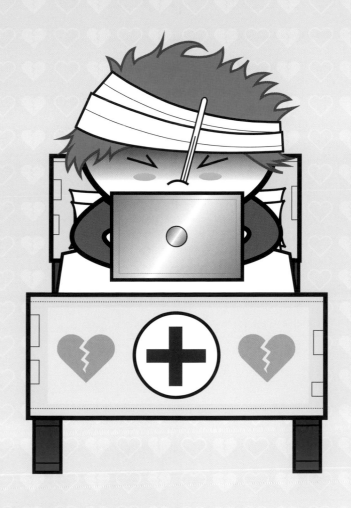

"I think I'm coming down with something."

The Boss

Weirdos and Losers

WHY YOU FELL FOR HIM

He was your boss. Or maybe your boss's boss. One night you were both working late and one thing led to another. You swore it wouldn't happen again. But it did.

WHY YOU SPLIT UP

Having a big secret stopped being fun when you realized you weren't fooling anyone. Not even his wife. It was the last straw when, to show how fair he was, he didn't promote you.

DESCRIPTION

Suit and tie by day, kinky by night. Older than you are, but not necessarily wiser. When a concerned friend convinces you to watch *The Secretary*, you have to turn it off.

NOT TO BE CONFUSED WITH

The Workaholic, The Office Romance, Midlife Crisis Man.

CHECKLIST

He's your boss ✔

Tears off your clothes, folds his neatly ✔

You don't go out, you stay in (the office) ✔

You'll never look at the photocopier the same way again ✔

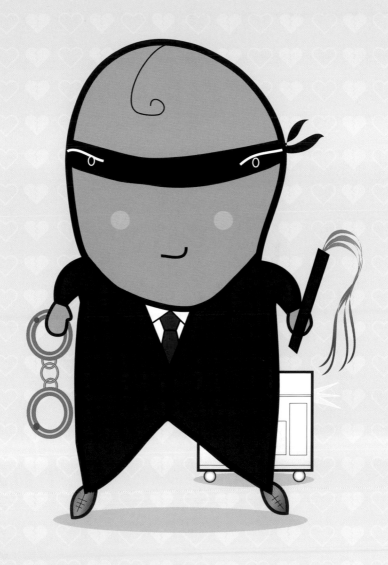

"Are you working late tonight?"

Tinder Time

Dating can be a minefield. Beware of The Tinder Addict (has a PhD in swiping), The Two-Timer (a.k.a. the champion cheater), and The Catfish (taking fiction to new levels). Have fun playing with The Boy Toy, but don't let your feelings get hurt by The Ghost—it's not you, it's him. Definitely him. These bootie-call buddies will keep you coming back for more until you decide enough is enough and pull the plug on a relationship that only ever had a chance in the bedroom.

The Hot Guy

Tinder Time

WHY YOU FELL FOR HIM

He was so gorgeous you couldn't take your eyes off him. You woke up in the middle of the night to watch him sleep. You knew looks shouldn't matter, but…

WHY YOU SPLIT UP

The trouble was, he knew he was hot. When you saw him watching himself in the mirror over his bed, you realized that he was more into himself than he was into you.

DESCRIPTION

Delicious kissable lips, perfect white teeth, cheekbones you could cut glass with, square jaw, cute little ears, smooth hard chest, and the rest! Totally yum.

NOT TO BE CONFUSED WITH

The Movie Star, The Model, A Peach Emoji.

CHECKLIST

The only content on his Instagram are selfies ✔

Uses more beauty products than you do ✔

Loves shopping–for himself, not for you ✔

Never passes a mirror without checking himself out ✔

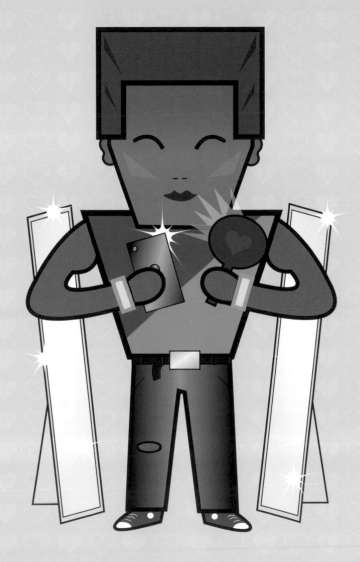

"I get James Dean a lot."

The Boy Toy

Tinder Time

WHY YOU FELL FOR HIM

What a cutie! You couldn't decide whether to unzip him or teach him to tie his shoelaces, but he was so hot you went for unzip. Excellent choice—he made you feel like the sexy older woman.

WHY YOU SPLIT UP

You took him out to dinner and the waiter thought you were his mom. You panicked. Sure, that's technically possible, but you couldn't really be his mom's age. Could you??? And yes, you always paid for dinner—and everything else. There was something wrong with this picture.

DESCRIPTION

Sneakers, jeans, T-shirt, hoodie, messy hair. Skateboard. Backpack. Beer pong is his favorite sport.

NOT TO BE CONFUSED WITH

Justin Bieber, A Puppy.

CHECKLIST

Definitely legal. (You checked his driver's license.) ✔

Uses so much slang you don't understand you bookmark UrbanDictionary.com ✔

Thinks Facebook is for old people ✔

Considers your favorite bands oldies ✔

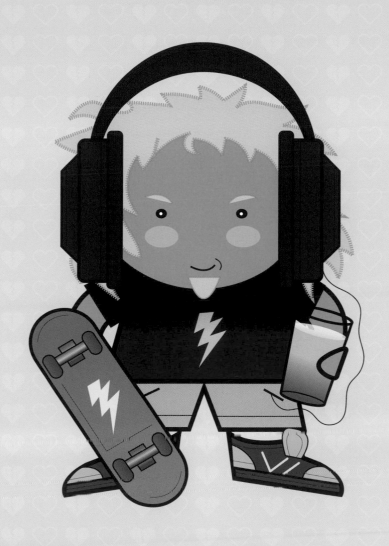

"Seriously? You're carding me?"

The Tinder Addict

Tinder Time

WHY YOU FELL FOR HIM

From the perfect profile picture to his carefully crafted personal bio, he checked all the boxes and exceeded expectation. Past Tinder dates, however, had set the bar pretty low.

WHY YOU SPLIT UP

You deleted all your dating apps but it turned out he didn't do the same. The relationship ended after you caught him swiping right when you got back from the ladies' room. You found out later that he'd hit on your best friend, her sister, and the new girl at work.

DESCRIPTION

Sweet and innocent looking but sneaky. Bikes everywhere so he can beat the traffic as he flits between dates. Drinks espresso martinis after dinner so he can stay up microcheating on you while you sleep.

NOT TO BE CONFUSED WITH

The Hot Guy, The Two-Timer.

CHECKLIST

Has arthritis in his thumb from swiping too much ✔

Takes such long bathroom breaks (with his phone) you think he's doing something weird in there ✔

A walking dictionary of Tinder slang ✔

Dating is basically his full-time job ✔

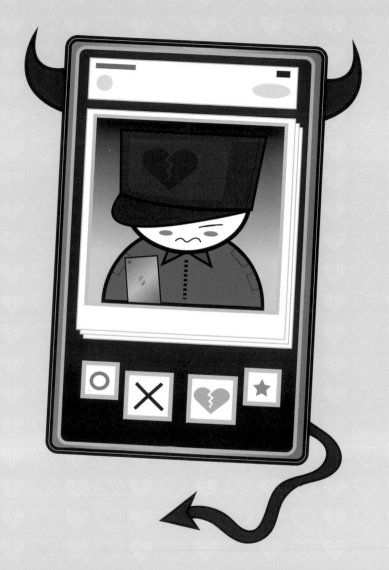

"I thought we weren't exclusive."

The Two-Timer

Tinder Time

WHY YOU FELL FOR HIM

He seemed so solid and steady, really reliable, and definitely husband material. And that was the problem. He was actually someone's husband, or at least fiancé, as you found out when she DM'd you. Eeek!

WHY YOU SPLIT UP

He tried to get you back with the usual "She doesn't understand me" BS. You weren't buying it. He might be a cheater, but you weren't.

DESCRIPTION

His phone pings all the time, even when you're in the hot tub. "Sorry, Babe, work." He goes outside to take calls. Work again. He disappears for days. Business trip. You start to wonder…

NOT TO BE CONFUSED WITH

The Polyamorous Guy, The Secret Agent.

CHECKLIST

Pale mark on his ring finger ✔

Always busy on weekends, over the holidays, and on Valentine's Day ✔

Never uses his card, always pays with cash ✔

Has two phones: the burner you phone him on and the "work" one ✔

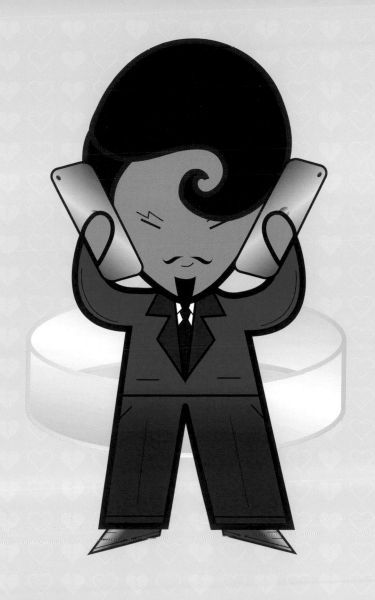

"We don't even sleep together anymore."

The Catfish

Tinder Time

WHY YOU FELL FOR HIM

You had a great relationship: nonstop texting; long, sexy messaging sessions. You even watched TV together, just not in the same room (or time zone, for all you know). The only problem was you've never met him IRL.

WHY YOU SPLIT UP

You arranged a date. He canceled at the last minute. You tried again. Another no show complete with weird excuse. If you ever did meet him, you found you've been catfished: his whole profile from his age to his picture was a lie.

DESCRIPTION

A foot shorter and a mile uglier than his profile picture.

NOT TO BE CONFUSED WITH

The Tinder Addict, A Real Person.

CHECKLIST

Makes up crazy excuses for why he can't meet you IRL ✓

His profile is too good to be true ✓

Your internet stalking efforts draw a blank ✓

Loves messaging; hates FaceTime ✓

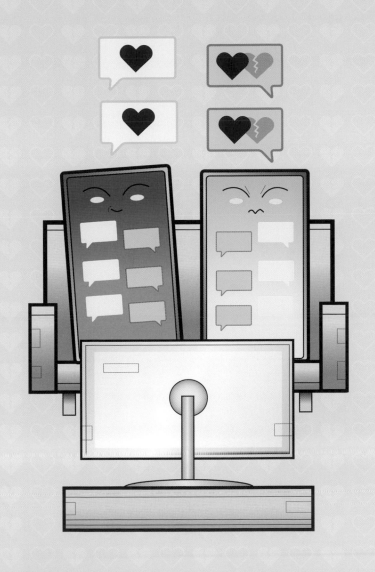

"Got to cancel. Abducted by aliens! LOL"

The Ghost

Tinder Time

WHY YOU FELL FOR HIM

Hard to remember as you are still furious that he disappeared without a word. Maybe even in mid–text or halfway through a date. Whether you were together for a week, a month, or even a year, you deserved a goodbye, at least.

WHY YOU SPLIT UP

One day, he just disappeared. At first, you were worried. Had he been offed by the mob? Eaten by zombies? Abducted by aliens? Kidnapped by a cult? Then it dawned: you'd been ghosted. Ouch.

DESCRIPTION

A big, blank space. The sound of silence. The invisible man. No matter how you slice it, he's gone, baby, gone.

NOT TO BE CONFUSED WITH

The Two-Timer, The Party Animal.

CHECKLIST

No phone, no email, no social media–all gone ✔

King of the vanishing act ✔

Like Casper the Ghost, but not at all friendly ✔

Leaves you wondering why ✔

"I'll be back in a few ..."

That Fatal Flaw

This bunch of bad boys isn't all bad, but each of them has a fatal flaw. From The Momma's Boy and Always a Teenager to such obsessives as The Workaholic and The Gym Rat, none of them are quite right. Although you fell hard for The Hipster and ached for The Activist, they didn't make the cut. They all had potential, if only it was for that one thing that drove you up the wall.

The Momma's Boy

That Fatal Flaw

WHY YOU FELL FOR HIM

He was attentive and adoring with you so you weren't surprised he was the same way with his mom. You assumed there was enough affection to go around.

WHY YOU SPLIT UP

Since her divorce, Saturday nights were reserved for mom. It was always Italian followed by the latest period piece. The routine got old fast. You didn't sign up to be the third wheel and you never liked Meryl Streep anyway.

DESCRIPTION

If his mom knits, he wears sweaters; if she's into macramé, so are his plants; if she embroiders, he's got more cute cushions than an old lady.

NOT TO BE CONFUSED WITH

Norman Bates, The Parents' Favorite.

CHECKLIST

Takes his mom to dinner on Valentine's Day

Messages her hourly

Refrigerator and freezer packed with Mom-made casseroles and pies

Does his laundry at her place on the weekends

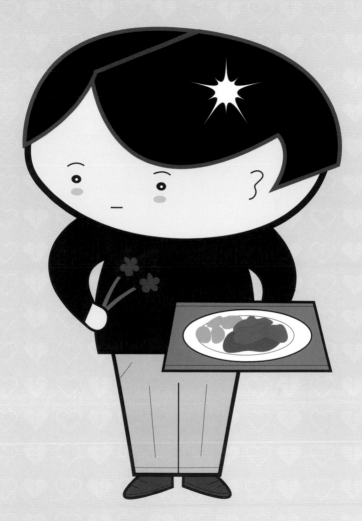

"You remind me of my mother. In a good way!"

Always a Teenager

That Fatal Flaw

WHY YOU FELL FOR HIM

You felt young and carefree with him. Making out in movie theaters, drinking forties out of paper bags on the street, riding on the back of his scooter. It was hot, rebellious, and sweet all at once.

WHY YOU SPLIT UP

His bedroom looked like a bomb had hit it—beer cans, pizza boxes, and roaches. You found panties under the bed (not yours—yuck!). Okay, they were from before you met, but seriously? You had too much self-respect for this man-child.

DESCRIPTION

Still dresses like he's seventeen, even though he's over thirty (way over). Ponytail. Scruffy T-shirt, board shorts, and tube socks uniform no matter the weather.

NOT TO BE CONFUSED WITH

Peter Pan, The Stoner, The Music Festival Fling.

CHECKLIST

Job? What job? ✔

Borrows money to buy you a drink ✔

Still hangs out with the gang from high school ✔

Owns more than one bong ✔

"I'm in the moment, babe!"

The Action Man

That Fatal Flaw

WHY YOU FELL FOR HIM

You loved the view from a hot-air balloon, thought skiing was fun, liked kayaking, didn't mind mountain biking, and were into his Ski-Doo.

WHY YOU SPLIT UP

This one was up for every known activity except staying in and chilling out. And after a while, you missed that. All that hiking, biking, windsurfing, and paragliding was wearing you out. And rock climbing was hell on your manicure.

DESCRIPTION

Dresses head to toe in Patagonia. He has more hats than your grandma and his shoe collection rivals yours with special footwear for every one of his many activities from polo to parkour, surfing to snowshoeing.

NOT TO BE CONFUSED WITH

The Jock, James Bond.

CHECKLIST

Loves getting down (and dirty)…on a Tough Mudder ✔

His basement looks like a sporting goods store ✔

Has a bike rack and a roof rack on his car ✔

Prefers sex in a sleeping bag to boning in a bed ✔

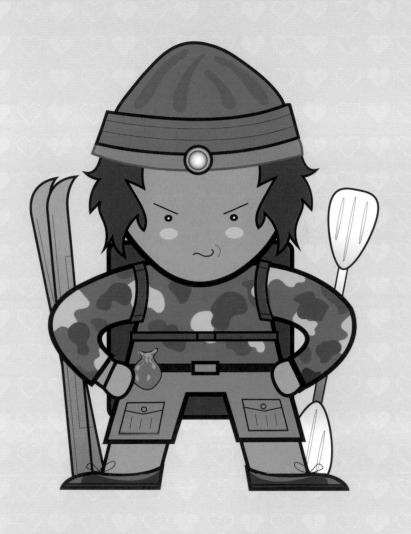

"Why don't we do it in the woods?"

The Activist

That Fatal Flaw

WHY YOU FELL FOR HIM

He looked so cool and was totally on message. He promised new possibilities such as changing the world (yes!), tantric sex (bring it on!), and veganism (not so much).

WHY YOU SPLIT UP

You love animals and believe in saving the environment but does that mean you can't fly/drive/wear new clothes/own nice shoes? Is it really true that the revolution doesn't need good hair? Tough choices had to be made. Ditching him wasn't the toughest.

DESCRIPTION

Dreads, scarves, beads, and steel-cap boots. Faint whiff of patchouli, or is that eau-de-second-hand clothes? Aspires to living in a yurt; actually lives in a grungy apartment.

NOT TO BE CONFUSED WITH

The Vegan, The Hipster.

CHECKLIST

So woke he doesn't need an alarm clock or coffee

Often found chained to trees, fences, earth-moving equipment

Owns a bullhorn, spray paint, Anonymous mask

Carries a copy of *The Communist Manifesto* in his back pocket

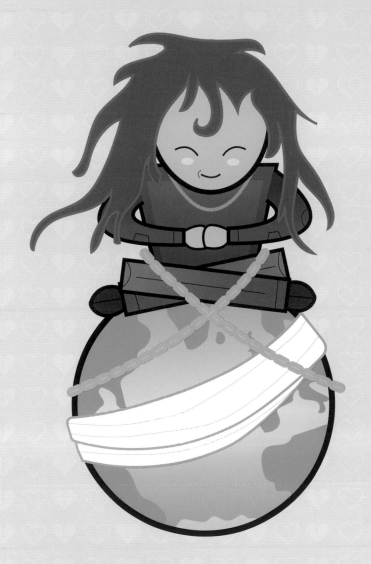

"Shop local, think global!"

The Hipster

That Fatal Flaw

WHY YOU FELL FOR HIM

You both rode fixed-gear bikes and only drank cold brew. His Instagram feed was an homage to avocado toast, Sriracha, and yes, his own man bun. He rolled you cigarettes, fixed your flat tires, and his sleeves were damn sexy.

WHY YOU SPLIT UP

Finding artisanal food near where you lived was tough and that's all he'd eat. The final straw was when you realized his hair was longer and his jeans were tighter than yours.

DESCRIPTION

Those horn-rimmed glasses, the giant earphones, the Carhart jacket, and the worn leather boots. He owns several beanies and sometimes wears more than one at once.

NOT TO BE CONFUSED WITH

The Activist, The Artist, Jake Gyllenhaal.

CHECKLIST

Even if he actually lives in Podunk, his heart's in Brooklyn

Beard maintenance takes twenty minutes morning and evening

Only listens to vinyl; owns a typewriter

Brews his own kombucha; ferments his own kimchi

"Where's this sourced?"

The Cheapskate

That Fatal Flaw

WHY YOU FELL FOR HIM

It was all going great until you read the dedication inside the book he gave you for Christmas: "To a Great Nephew." #regifted

WHY YOU SPLIT UP

You got tired of driving miles out of your way to get the cheapest gas, sneaking the waitress extra money because he was too tight to tip, fighting for a table at the early bird special, and spending Saturday nights clipping coupons. The last straw? When he took the bottle of wine he brought to your friend's party back home with him.

DESCRIPTION

His clothes are always an odd color (lavender jeans?). His apartment is furnished with random stuff from factory clearance showrooms, but his savings account is doing very well, thanks.

NOT TO BE CONFUSED WITH

The Parents' Favorite, The Accountant.

CHECKLIST

Always gets the doggie bag when you eat out ✔

Loves a sale; never pays full price ✔

Pockets packets of sugar, creamer, ketchup, and even butter. Ew! ✔

Plots his spending on a spreadsheet and updates hourly ✔

"Let's go Dutch."

The Nerd
That Fatal Flaw

WHY YOU FELL FOR HIM

Those big black-rimmed glasses magnified his eyes. He was so smart—your own walking Wikipedia. His love of romance languages was charming but you were soon bored by the vocab quizzes.

WHY YOU SPLIT UP

He corrected your pronunciation and grammar. In English. But for all his linguistic prowess, he didn't know how to use his tongue where it mattered the most.

DESCRIPTION

Wears the same clothes he wore in high school. They don't fit, but he's too busy rereading *Beowulf* to care. Uses a pocket protector. Wears wing tips and ironic science T-shirts, but without the irony.

NOT TO BE CONFUSED WITH

The Momma's Boy, The Hipster, The Fixer Upper.

CHECKLIST

Makes Sheldon from *The Big Bang Theory* seem warm and fuzzy ✔

Loves dictionaries, encyclopedias, and first editions ✔

Owns an abacus, a slide rule, and a wall chart of the periodic table ✔

Never wants to party; always up for Trivial Pursuit ✔

"I read a book on that…"

The Workaholic

That Fatal Flaw

WHY YOU FELL FOR HIM

He brought his perfectionism, drive, and work ethic to wooing you. Once you were together, he encouraged you to dream big, work harder, and go for that promotion. That gave him more time to work and made you half of a power couple! Win–win.

WHY YOU SPLIT UP

Broken dates, long lonely weekends, and interrupted vacations. When you realized that the only thing not working was your relationship, you said goodbye. Just then his phone pinged and you left as he took yet another call.

DESCRIPTION

Sharp suits, crisp shirts, shoes that look handmade. Expensive haircut and luggage.

NOT TO BE CONFUSED WITH

The Tycoon, Christian Grey.

CHECKLIST

Keeps a change of clothes at the office in case he sleeps there ✔

Holds the company record for rolled over vacation days ✔

Cell phone glued to his ear; never more than two feet from his laptop ✔

Loves spreadsheets and databases more than he loves you ✔

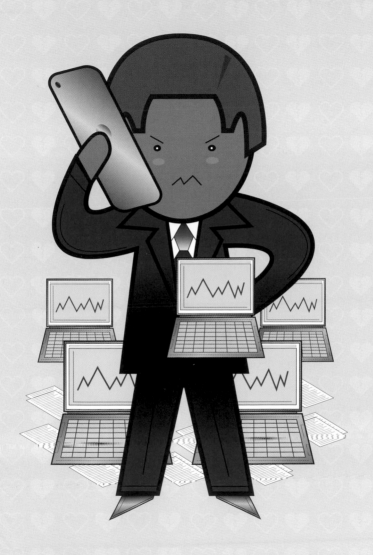

"I've just got to finish this report..."

The Gym Rat
That Fatal Flaw

WHY YOU FELL FOR HIM

Tanned, toned, and totally fit—what's not to like? Keeping a great bod great was a full-time job. Sunday was for batch cooking and every day was for working out. No exceptions! A vacation or even a weekend away was impossible.

WHY YOU SPLIT UP

This guy was so into numbers (mainly his BMI) he could have been an accountant. He had spreadsheets on everything: steps walked, weights lifted, calories in, calories out. He probably had a more intimate relationship with his FitBit than with you.

DESCRIPTION

Athleisure is too casual for this guy. Bring on the muscle tank. Everyone at the gym knows him for his emphatic grunts and the deafening noise of his AC/DC-heavy workout playlist.

NOT TO BE CONFUSED WITH

The Jock, The Marathon Runner.

CHECKLIST

Leaves a trail of Blender Bottles everywhere he goes ✔

Never passes a mirror without checking out his abs ✔

Brings the gym home: kettlebells, jump ropes, pull-up bar in doorway ✔

Works out for two hours, and that's just in the morning ✔

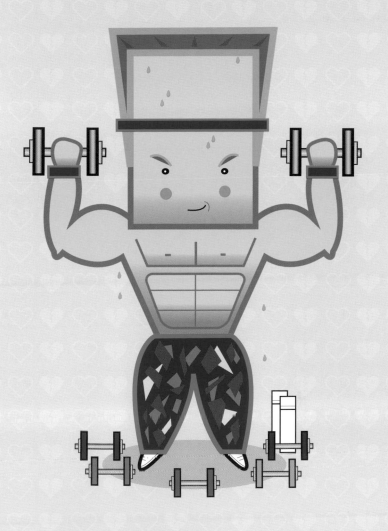

"Let me just show you this lift."

Mr. Long Distance

That Fatal Flaw

WHY YOU FELL FOR HIM

He was your bae; the only problem was that he was too far away. You'd racked up the air miles, spent Saturday nights alone, and took phone sex to new levels. Distance makes the heart grow fonder, right?

WHY YOU SPLIT UP

When it was Valentine's Day and you were having dinner together (on FaceTime) for the third year in a row, you both decided enough was enough. You cried, but not as much as you thought you would.

DESCRIPTION

Spends so much time in the airport that people think he works at TSA—he's on a first-name basis with the guys at curbside check-in, buys your birthday presents at Hudson News, and knows all the shortcuts through baggage claim.

NOT TO BE CONFUSED WITH

The Vacation Hottie, The French Exchange Student.

CHECKLIST

Lives in a different time zone, maybe even on a different continent ✔

Writes actual love letters and sends them in the mail ✔

The film of your life is *Planes, Trains, and Automobiles*, but it's not funny ✔

Sends you flowers for your birthday because he can't be there–again ✔

"I'm on standby. Got to go."

Still Stuck on his Ex

That Fatal Flaw

WHY YOU FELL FOR HIM

You were both on the rebound and being together made sense. He got your sensitivities, knew not to ask too many questions, and also listened to Adele on repeat. Misery loves company, right?

WHY YOU SPLIT UP

He talked so much about his ex that you could have aced a trivia round all about her. At first, you thought he was just getting over the breakup and cut him some slack, but finally you had to cut him loose.

DESCRIPTION

His favorite sweater is one she gave him; he won't take the pictures from their vacation to Paris off the refrigerator; he still has his mail delivered to her apartment and goes every weekend to pick it up.

NOT TO BE CONFUSED WITH

The Married Guy, The Two-Timer.

CHECKLIST

The engagement ring hidden in his sock drawer? It's not for you ✓

Wells up when he hears their song on the radio ✓

Obsesses over his ex's social media feeds ✓

Calls you by her name in bed ✓

"She was just the best."

The Bachelor
That Fatal Flaw

WHY YOU FELL FOR HIM

You clicked in all the ways that mattered and you were disarmed by his charm even if he refused to DTR. Whenever you talked about the future, he told you to live in the moment. And, damn, the moment with him was nice. Sexy texts at all hours of the day and night. Cocktails at sunset. A single rose. Just no ring.

WHY YOU SPLIT UP

You thought you could change him. You weren't needy like his last girlfriend, demanding like the one before, or neurotic like the one before that. Spot a pattern? Yup, he was the one with the problem.

DESCRIPTION

You know he owns a tux but he refuses to be your plus-one. He loves to be with you—until you want a future—even a short-term one.

NOT TO BE CONFUSED WITH

The Tinder Addict, The Polyamorous Guy.

CHECKLIST

Has a commitment phobia; he should get therapy ✔

Won't change his status to "in a relationship" even though you've been dating for months ✔

Mention meeting your parents and he chokes ✔

Likes to be the only single guy at the wedding ✔

"I don't like labels."

The Keepers

You know he's Mr. Right because he puts you before anything or anyone else. If he's The Fiancé, he puts a ring on it, but true love doesn't always end with a walk down the aisle. Take The Life Partner; you're good together and you're married in all but name, plus you've got the kitties, and sometimes even the kids, to prove it. Whichever one is your keeper, you know you've got the best of the bunch.

The Life Partner

The Keepers

WHY YOU FELL FOR HIM

This wasn't the first rodeo for either of you—you'd both been burned by past relationships. You bonded over your "Fuck the wedding industrial complex!" bumper stickers. He helped you rediscover stability, love, and hope.

WHY YOU SPLIT UP

You didn't! You moved in together and got a cat, then another. It made financial sense to get on his health insurance, so you did that, too. People started introducing you as husband and wife. Eventually, you stopped correcting them. After all, he was your forever partner.

DESCRIPTION

A Hawaiian shirt and black jeans are his idea of wedding attire. Keeps a framed copy of the holiday card of you, him, and the cats in Santa hats on his desk at work. Refers to you as the "Kitty Mama."

NOT TO BE CONFUSED WITH

Still Stuck on his Ex, The Fiancé.

CHECKLIST

Splits everything with you 50-50, even after decades ✓

Insists on separate bank accounts ✓

Has an eclectic collection of jewelry, but no gold band ✓

Loves other people's kids, but swears he doesn't want any of his own ✓

"Let's not get married."

The Lifer

The Keepers

WHY YOU FELL FOR HIM

You've been together so long you can't remember why you fell in love with him or who you even are without him. And that's a little scary. The thrill has gone, but he's like a giant hot water bottle or a big security blanket. You can't let go.

WHY YOU SPLIT UP

You didn't. The forces of inertia are holding you too tight. Everyone else thinks it's time for you two to buy a house, get married, or have a baby, but you secretly want to split up and suspect he does, too.

DESCRIPTION

He's like the old sweats he puts on every night when he gets home from work: warm, cozy, and gray.

NOT TO BE CONFUSED WITH

The High School Boyfriend, The First Love.

CHECKLIST

Like an old Labrador retriever: loyal, dependable, and farts in bed ✓

Knows how to fix your car, your computer, and the furnace ✓

Forgets your birthday, your anniversary, and Valentine's Day ✓

Has had an engagement ring hidden in his sock drawer for five years ✓

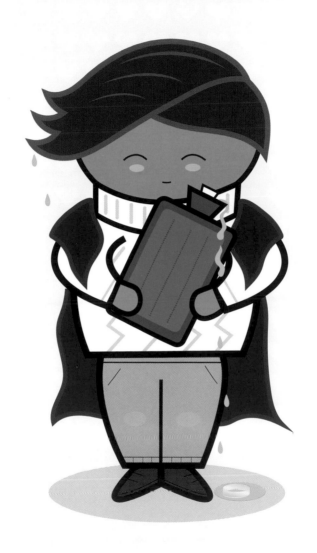

"You know I love you, why do I have to say it?"

The Fiancé

The Keepers

WHY YOU FELL FOR HIM

Cue the Etta James. At last, your love has come along. He's the yin to your yang and your best friend in the whole world. When he proposed, he even got down on one knee. You cried.

WHY YOU SPLIT UP

You didn't! You're engaged! (Although you had some pretty intense arguments about the wedding plans.)

DESCRIPTION

Tux with a boutonniere because marriage is serious stuff; Keds and dark glasses to keep it real.

NOT TO BE CONFUSED WITH

The Bae, The Lifer.

CHECKLIST

Takes you ring shopping then surprises you with the perfect ring ✓

Pops the question at the Eiffel Tower ✓

Hires a videographer to secretly film the proposal ✓

Has champagne on ice all ready for your first toast ✓

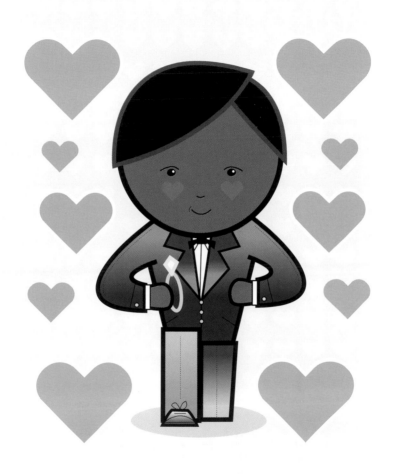

"I want to spend the rest of my life with you."

Checklist

The Action Man	♥	The Jealous Guy	♥
The Activist	♥	The Jock	♥
Always a Teenager	♥	The Lead Guitarist	♥
The Bachelor	♥	The Life Partner	♥
The Boss	♥	The Lifer	♥
The Boy Toy	♥	Mr. Long Distance	♥
The Catfish	♥	The Mansplainer	♥
The Cheapskate	♥	Midlife Crisis Man	♥
The Collector	♥	The Momma's Boy	♥
The Couch Potato	♥	The Neat Freak	♥
DJ Devil	♥	The Nerd	♥
The Feeder	♥	The Parents' Favorite	♥
The Fiancé	♥	The Party Animal	♥
The Fixer Upper	♥	Mr. Sad in the Sack	♥
The Gamer	♥	The Stalker	♥
The Ghost	♥	Still Stuck on his Ex	♥
The Gym Rat	♥	The Tinder Addict	♥
The Hipster	♥	Too Into Your Mom	♥
The Hot Guy	♥	The Two-Timer	♥
The Hypochondriac	♥	The Workaholic	♥